I'm Mark and I'm fed up. Mum has a new boyfriend.

Dad left two years ago.
I still see him every other week, but it's not the same. I miss him.
Mum and Dad used to argue a lot.
Mum said that they just didn't get on any more.
I hope it was nothing to do with me.

3

Marlon is round here all the time.
He always wants to play football. I think he wants to show me up.
I'm no good at football, I'm a swimmer.
Mum says I have to give him a chance.
Well I don't see why.

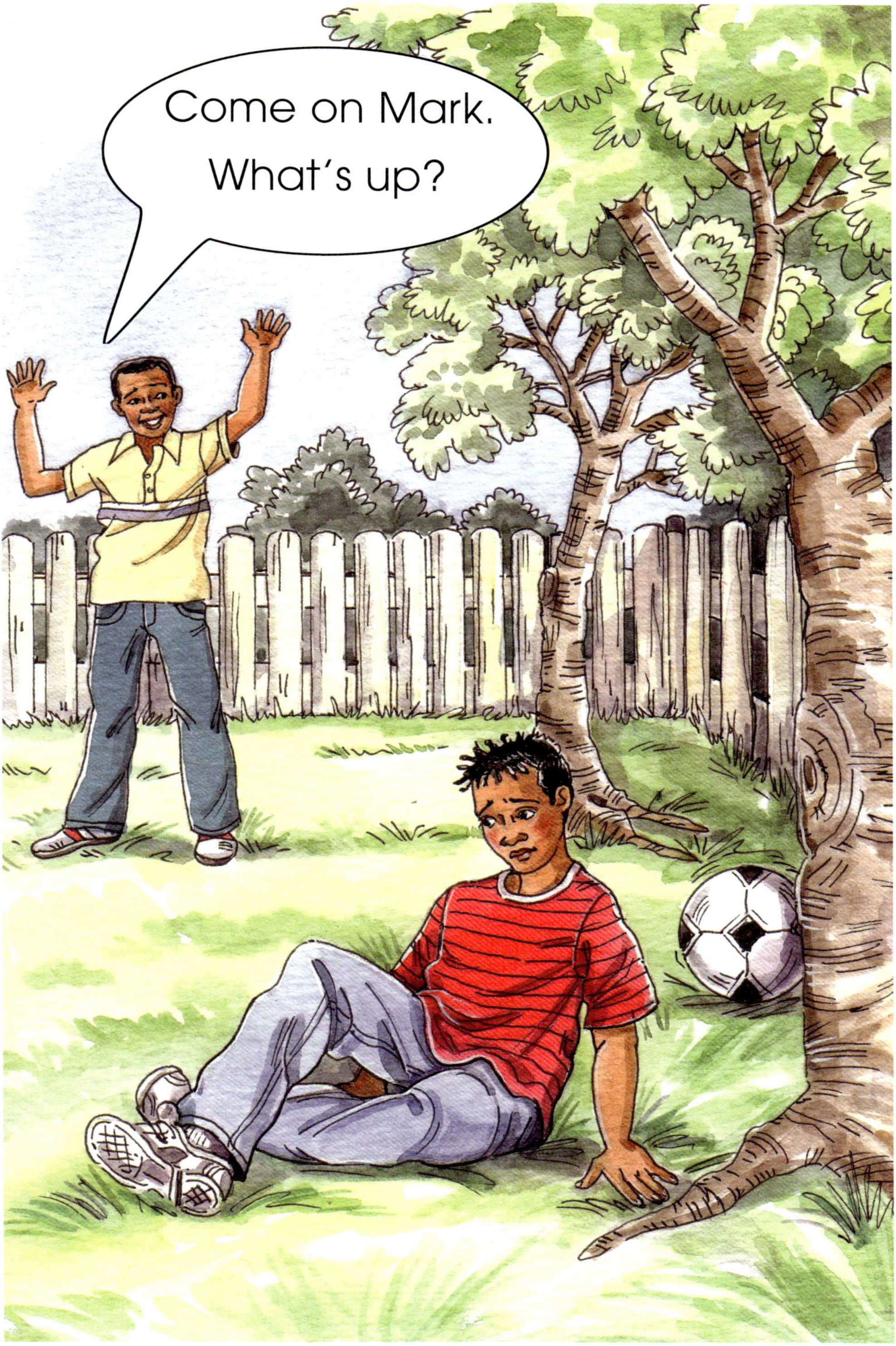
Come on Mark.
What's up?

Last night Marlon wanted to watch the football on TV. So Mum switched channels.
She always does what he wants.
She knows I watch *Coronation Street*.
She doesn't care about me any more.
She just wants to please Marlon.

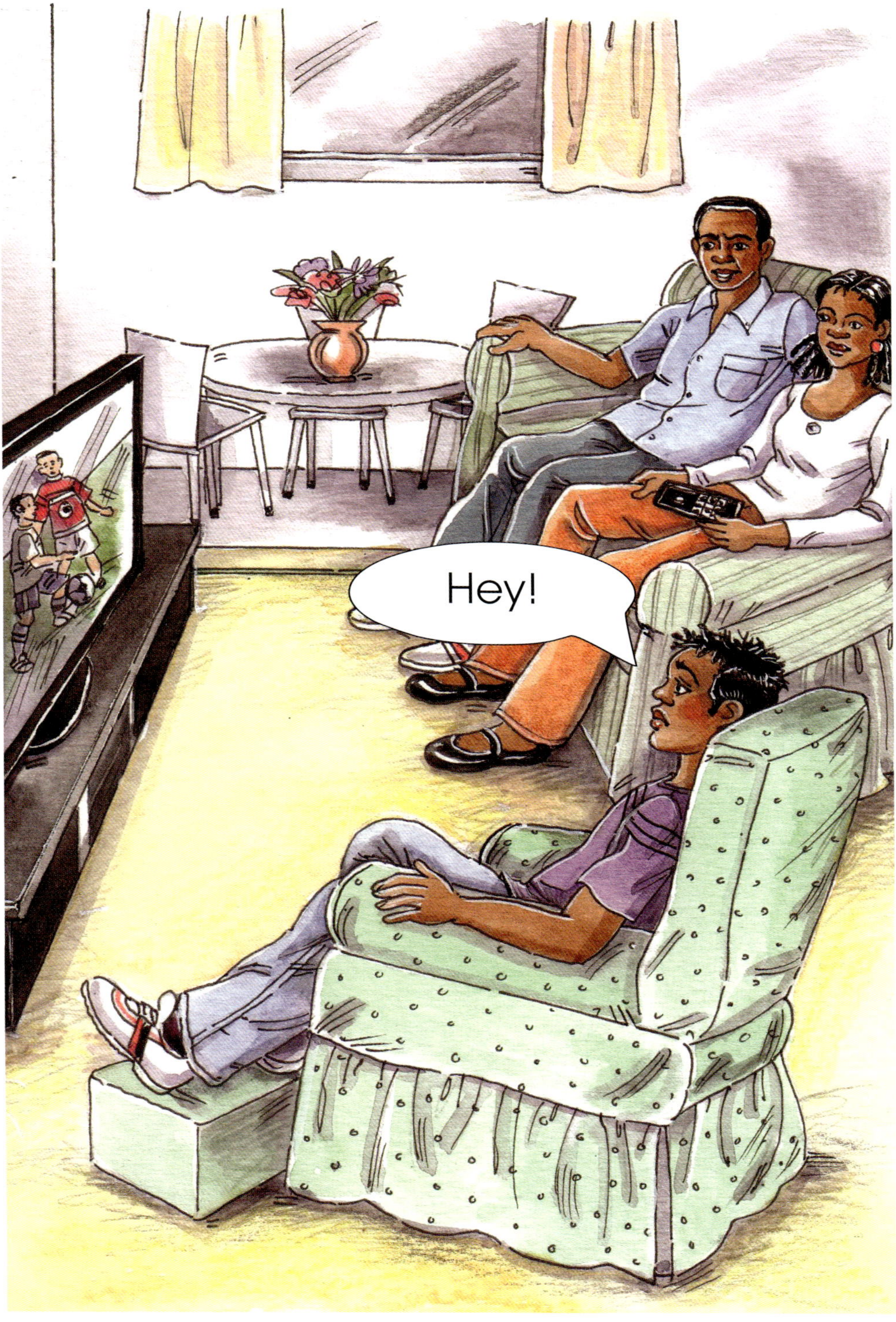
Hey!

We never watch TV together any more.
Mum just watches football and films with Marlon.
They cuddle up on the sofa. It's really embarrassing.
I feel left out.

9

When I get in from college Marlon always asks me what I've been doing.
What's it got to do with him?
It's none of his business.
Mum says Marlon is trying to be friendly.

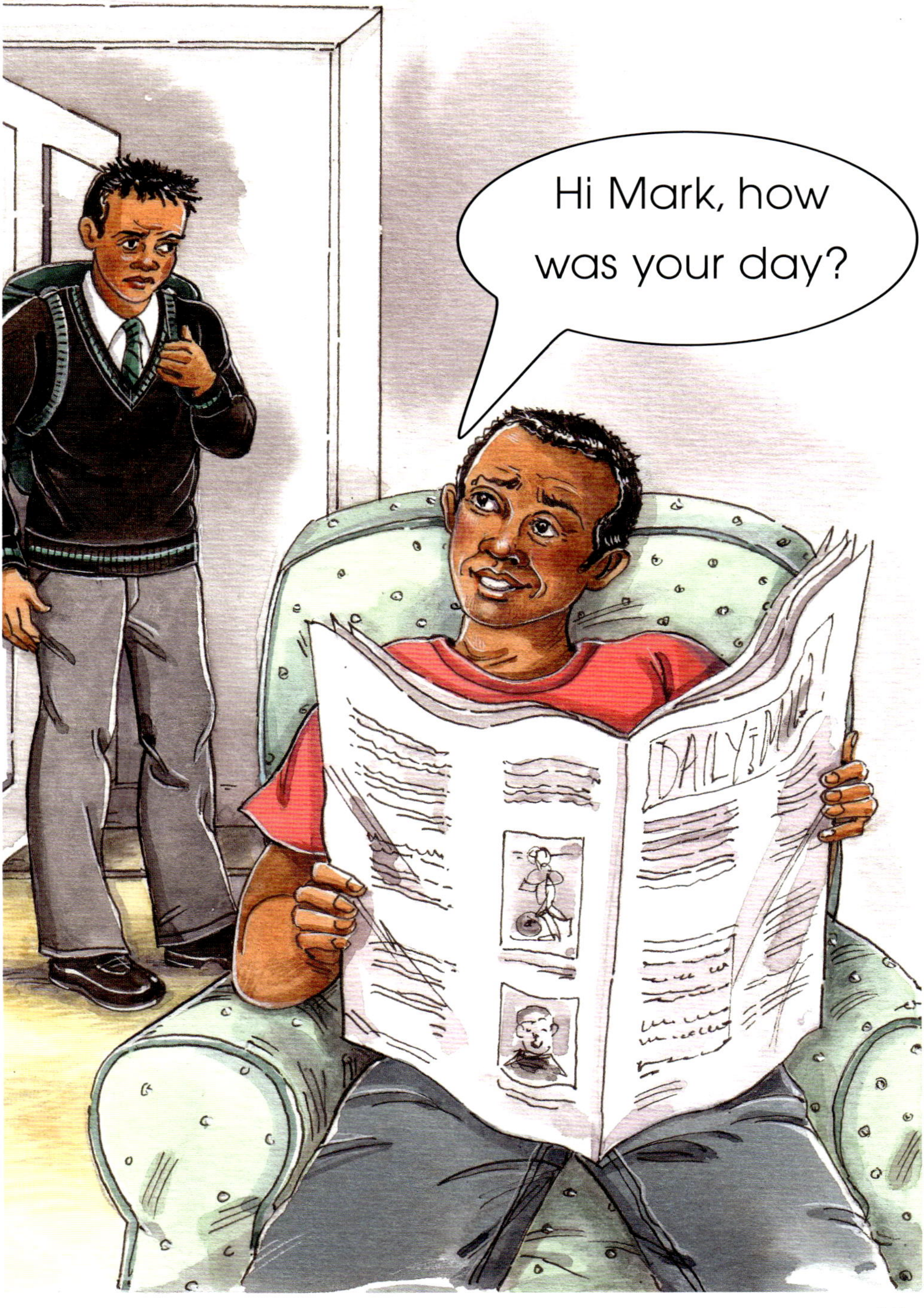
Hi Mark, how was your day?
DAILY MAIL

Last night Mum called up the stairs, "Tea's ready. Marlon's not coming round tonight."

"I don't care. And I don't want any tea," I said.

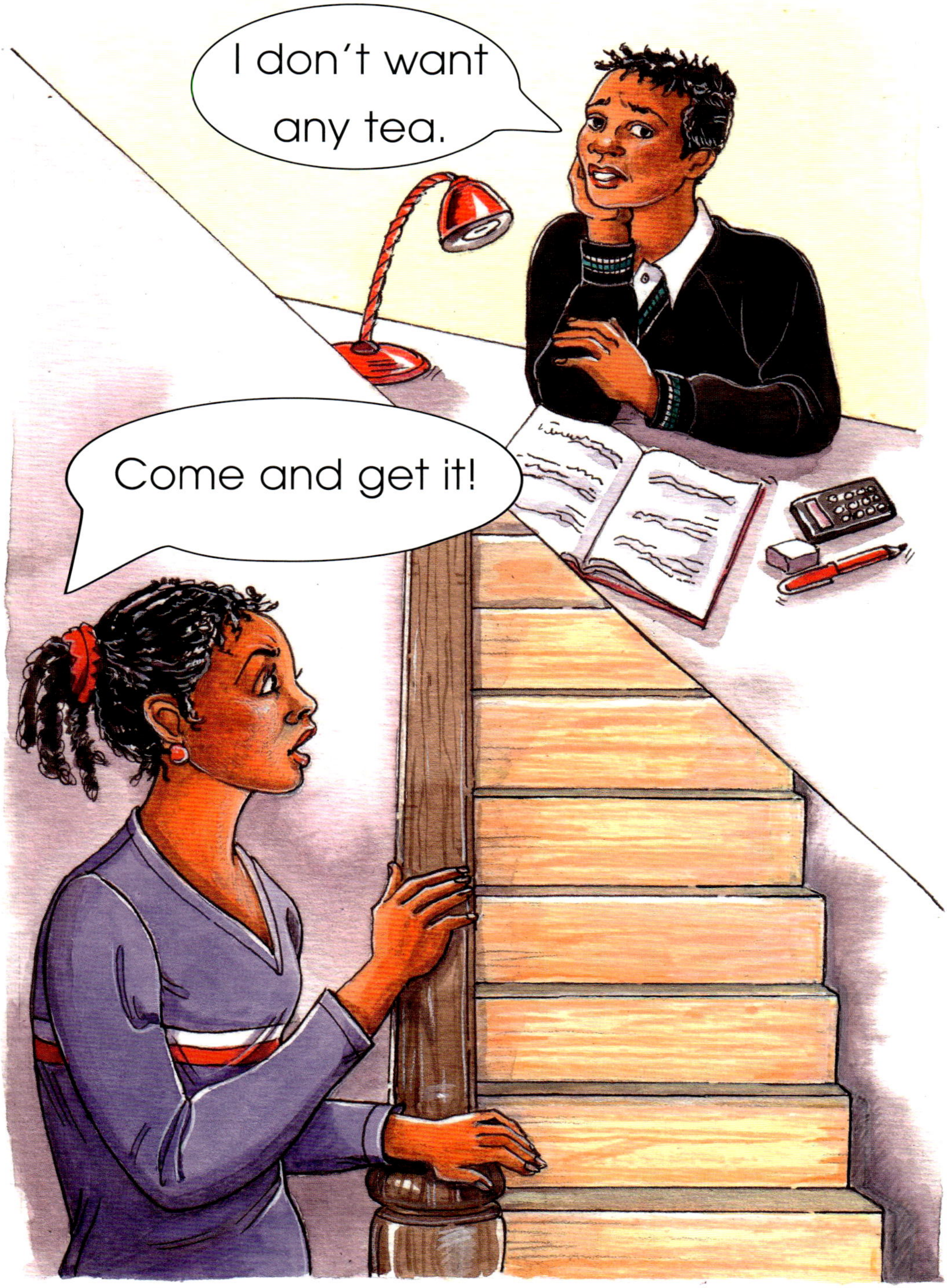
I don't want any tea.
Come and get it!

Later we talked.

"Marlon's here to stay," Mum said. "He doesn't want to take Dad's place. He just wants to be friends."

Mum says we are going swimming together at the weekend. She says Marlon isn't good at swimming. He's only coming to be nice to me.

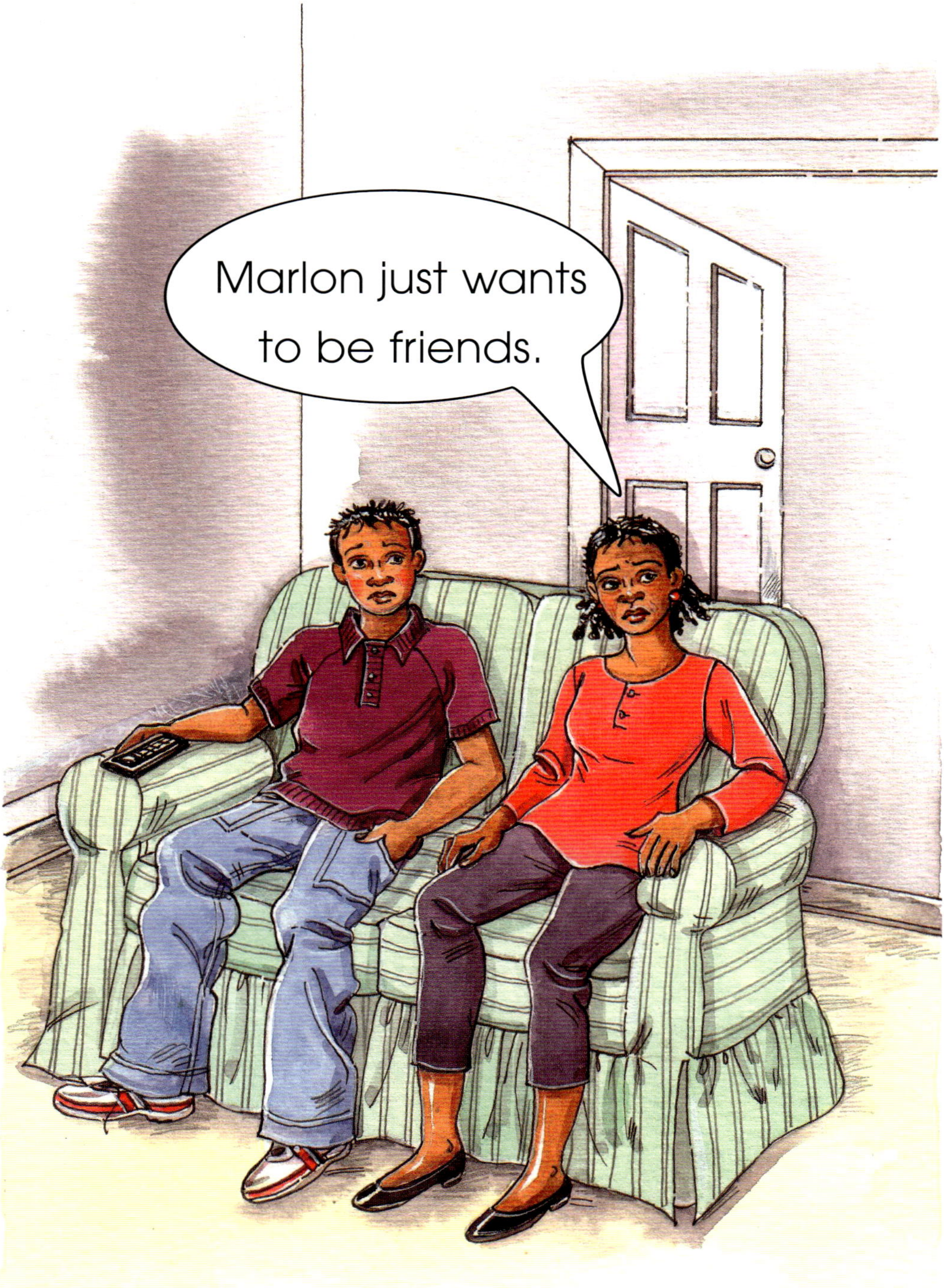
Marlon just wants to be friends.

Mum's right. Marlon's useless!
He doesn't know how to swim.
Perhaps I could help him . . .